# GRACE HAPPENS

## STUDY GUIDE

**40**
**DAYS**
*of*
**GRACE**

RICK LONG

# CONTENTS

GRACE HAPPENS

INTRODUCTION

This may sound like an unbelievably elementary discovery, but over the years I've found that many people never become the person God actually created them to be. There are one million different reasons why, but they can all be traced back to one major issue: they have failed to see that *Grace Happens*. God's grace is instantaneous and constant. God's grace carries every person through life's changes whether they are a believer or not. Without God's grace, we would not have air in our lungs and our heart would stop beating.

This series is for everyone. During the sessions, you'll hear some incredible stories of many people whose lives have been transformed by the grace of God. Stories that include subjects like suicide, divorce, loss of a child, loss of a job, sickness, and broken relationships. You'll learn about the countless failures and mistakes I made along the way, as well as a few things I managed to get right. You will see how God's grace can take an average "Joe"(or Rick in my case), and use any one of them to make a difference in the world.

Your small group presents a unique opportunity. Whether you are a stay at home parent, business executive, doctor, janitor, truck driver, pastor, missionary, or a student with no idea where you're going in life, these sessions will help you move towards answering the most important questions in life: Why are you on this earth? Does God really exist and does he truly have a plan for your life? And the most important question you'll answer this side of eternity, "Can I know for sure, beyond a shadow of a doubt that I will go to heaven when I die?"

My hope is that this series will encourage your spiritual maturity and prepare you for life's challenges, victories and defeats. Besides the weekly sessions, you will also find daily Scriptures to guide you, and questions for reflection.

I believe there is nothing greater than the fact that Grace happens, especially as it manifests itself in so many different aspects of our life. I have distinguished between six categories of grace, which are purely based on my own experience. There are probably many others. We start with **Simple Grace**, which is the amazing grace of God that brings us to salvation. **Constant Grace** is the undercurrent of God's grace that motivates and sustains us on a daily basis. When we suffer pain and loss, **Comforting Grace** gives us hope even in the face of life's storms. **Fearless Grace** stands by our side as we face the many challenges the world places before us, and helps us live a victorious life. **Selfless Grace** demonstrates how we are to care for the people around us, and is a key step toward living a fulfilled life. We'll close with **Daring Grace**, which inspires unexpected boldness to change the world, starting with the person right in front of you.

The word "Happens" has been preceded by many different nouns and pronouns: life happens, poop happens, pain happens, joy happens. But I firmly believe there is only one word which truly can be used

with this phrase—*Grace Happens*. Because the only constant in the universe is God's grace.

As I move into my fourth decade in ministry as a pastor, I have discovered how little I actually understand God's grace, and how much more of it I actually need. My prayer is that over the course of these sessions you will find a greater understanding of God's grace in your life, and discover how his grace can direct you along a path of greater significance and purpose than you could ever have imagined.

Thanks for joining us.
**Pastor Rick Long**

GRACE HAPPENS

40 DAYS OF GRACE

# USING
# THIS
# STUDY
# GUIDE

**(Tools to Help You Have a Great Small Group Experience!)**

1.  Notice in the Table of Contents there are three sections: (1) Sessions; (2) Appendices; and (3) Small Group Leaders. Familiarize yourself with the Appendices. Some of them will be used in the sessions themselves.

2.  If you are facilitating/leading or co-leading a small group, the section Small Group Leaders will give you some experiences of others that will encourage you and help you avoid many common obstacles to effective small group leadership.

3.  Use this as a guide, not a straightjacket. If the group responds to the lesson in an unexpected but honest way, go with that. If you think of a better question than the next one in the lesson, ask it. Take to heart the insights included in the Frequently Asked Questions pages and the Small Group Leaders section.

4.  Enjoy your Small Group experience.

5.  Pray before each session—for your group members, for your time together, for wisdom and insights.

6.  Read the Outline for Each Session on the next pages so that you understand how the sessions will flow.

# OUTLINE
# OF
# EACH
# SESSION

Most people want to live a life that is orderly, meaningful, and satisfying, but few achieve this by themselves. And most small groups struggle to balance all of God's purposes in their meetings. Groups tend to overemphasize one of the various reasons for meeting. Rarely is there a healthy balance that includes teaching, evangelism, ministry, practical experiences, and worship. That's why we've included these elements in this study, so you can practice together living a healthy, balanced spiritual life over time.

A typical group session for the *Grace Happens – 40 Days of Grace* study will include the following:

## THEME

The lessons we will learn during *Grace Happens – 40 Days of Grace* are best illustrated in the lives of real people. Each session's teaching will include comments by real people reflecting on the significance of the theme for that session in their own lives.

## COMING TOGETHER

You have a story and your story of life change can be the most powerful tool God will use to touch others in your group and further his work in your own life. Here are a few questions to help you shape your story.

1  What did you think about God before becoming a believer? (If you're not a believer, share what you think now and don't be afraid. We all have questions about God.)

2  When did you become a believer in Jesus Christ? (Share some details about that moment in your life. I was in church, a youth group, a Christian event, or somewhere on your own.)

3  Now that you are a believer in Jesus Christ, what changes have you experienced and how have you seen God's grace in your life?

It definitely takes some courage to share your story, but don't be afraid. Remember that you're in the midst of people who love Jesus. If you can't talk about your story with those who love Jesus, then you'll never share your story with those who don't.

If you're uncomfortable sharing your story with the group, maybe share with one or two of the people you have made a stronger connection with during the small group. This type of sharing allows your group to go deeper and wider during discussions, prayer time, and even the moments when you just need encouragement.

As your group begins, use the Small Group Agreement and Small Group Calendar to help your group begin to build community. As the group develops intimacy, use the Spiritual Partner's Check-In Page

and the Prayer and Praise Report to keep the group connected.

### LEARNING TOGETHER/VIDEO TEACHING SEGMENT

Serving as a companion to the *Grace Happens – 40 Days of Grace* small group study guide is the *Grace Happens – 40 Days of Grace* video teaching. These videos combine teaching segments with leadership insights and personal stories of life change. Using the teaching video will add value to this 6-week commitment of doing life together and discovering how walking with Christ changes everything.

(NOTE: Questions with a * indicate the crucial ones to use if time is short)

### GROWING TOGETHER

In this section, your group will process the teaching from the video curriculum. The focus won't be on accumulating information, but on how we should live in light of the Word of God. We want to help you apply the insights from Scripture practically, creatively, and from your heart as well as your head. At the end of the day, allowing the timeless truths from God's Word to transform our lives in Christ is our greatest aim.

### DEEPER BIBLE STUDY

If you have time and want to dig deeper into more Bible passages about the topic at hand, we've provided additional passages and questions, which you can use either during the meeting or as homework. Your group may choose to read and prepare before each meeting in order to cover more biblical

material. Or, group members can use the Deeper Bible Study section during the week after the meeting. If you prefer not to do study homework, this section will provide you with plenty to discuss within the group. These options allow individuals or the whole group to expand their study while still accommodating those who can't do homework or are new to your group.

## SHARING TOGETHER

Here is where the Bible is urging us to "be doers of the Word, not just hearers" (James 1:22). Many people skip over this aspect of the Christian life because it's scary, relationally awkward, or simply too much work for their busy schedules. But Jesus wanted all of his disciples to help outsiders connect with him, to know him personally, and to carry out his commands. This doesn't necessarily mean preaching on street corners. It could mean welcoming a few newcomers into your group, hosting a short-term group in your home, or walking through this teaching with a friend. During this time, you'll have an opportunity to go beyond Bible study to biblical living.

## GOING TOGETHER

We have Jesus' affirmation that every aspect of life can ultimately be measured as a way of fulfilling one or both of the "bottom line" commandments: Love God and Love others. (Mark 12:29–31 NIV). The group session will close with time for personal response to God and group prayer, seeking to keep this crucial commandment before us at all times.

This is a good place to have different group members close in prayer, even when the instructions don't specify. You can also provide some time if the schedule allows for people to reflect on their Prayer and

GRACE HAPPENS 40 DAYS OF GRACE

Praise Report or take a little time to meet with a Spiritual Partner.

## DAILY DEVOTIONALS

In the Daily Devotionals pages, you will have a chance to slow down, read just a small portion of scripture each day, and reflect and pray through it. You'll then have an opportunity to journal your response to what you've read. Note that the daily devotionals are numbered 1-42 to match the companion book to this series called *Grace Happens,* which is full of stories that illustrate many of the teaching lessons in these sessions. Use this section to seek God on your own throughout the week. This time at home should begin and end with prayer. Don't get in a hurry; take enough time to hear God's direction.

## WEEKLY MEMORY VERSE

For each session we have provided a memory verse that emphasizes an important truth from the session. This is an optional exercise, but we believe that memorizing Scripture can be a vital part of filling our minds with God's will for our lives. We encourage you to give this important habit a try.

GRACE HAPPENS

# SIMPLE GRACE

Welcome to *Grace Happens – 40 Days of Grace*! I hope you are ready for an exploration of grace, God's grace. Let me tell you that I've met a lot of people who when they heard about God's grace immediately thought that could never happen to me; that they could never receive unconditional, freely offered grace. I've even been a person like that! But here's the thing that's amazing about grace; those who fully comprehend that they don't deserve grace are those who appreciate it the most when God graciously provides it. And the giving all starts with the one thing we all share, we are all sinners. Grace happens, even and especially when we don't expect it.

# COMING
# TOGETHER

During each session, we will begin with a question or brief activity designed to "put us on the same page" for the session. Since this is your first time together (at least for this new series), take a few minutes to make sure everyone knows names. You may want to review briefly the Small Group Agreement and Calendar from the Appendices. Also, here are a few housekeeping matters:

1   As you begin, take time to pass around a copy of the Small Group Roster on page 134, a sheet of paper, or one of your study guides opened to the Small Group Roster. Have everyone write down their contact information. Ask someone to make copies or type up a list with everyone's information and email it to the group this week.

2   Whether your group is new or ongoing, it's always important to reflect on and review your values together. On page 128 is a Small Group Agreement with the values we've found most useful in sustaining healthy, balanced groups. We recommend that you choose one or two values—ones you haven't previously focused on or have room to grow in—to emphasize during this study. Choose ones that will take your group to the next stage of intimacy and spiritual health.

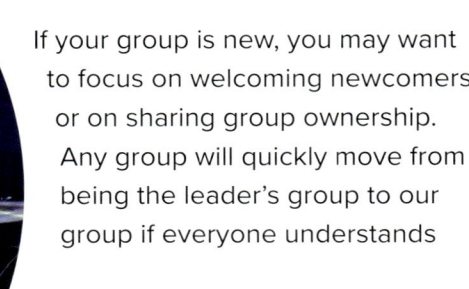

If your group is new, you may want to focus on welcoming newcomers or on sharing group ownership. Any group will quickly move from being the leader's group to our group if everyone understands the goals of the group and shares a small role.

We recommend that you rotate host homes on a regular basis and let the hosts lead the meeting. We've come to realize that healthy groups rotate leadership. This helps to develop every member's ability to shepherd a few people in a safe environment. Even Jesus gave others the opportunity to serve alongside him (Mark 6:30–44). Look at the FAQs on page 125 for additional information about hosting or leading the group.

*3  WARM UP: As you can tell by the title of this series, we actually believe grace happens. And most of us have some idea about what grace is and how to spot it in action. So let's take turns describing a situation or experience where we believe we saw grace in action.

4  WARM UP: Simple Grace has a lot to do with failures. What would be some funny or serious examples of colossal failures?

# LEARNING
# TOGETHER

Throughout the sessions in Grace Happens — 40 Days of Grace, we're going to be hearing some pointed teaching from Pastor Rick Long as well as some stories from people who have experienced the many ways God pours out His grace. And we need to be ready to share chapters from our stories, too.

# WATCH
## THE VIDEO

## SESSION 1

Use the space provided on the next page for notes, questions and comments you want to bring up in the discussion later.

# GROWING TOGETHER

After watching the video, the following questions will help you review and expand on the teaching you just experienced. Have a volunteer read the questions and facilitate the discussion among the group.

1   How would you explain simple grace based on what you just experienced during the video?


2   Pastor Rick pointed out that we ought to consider two possibilities before we throw Peter under the bus as someone who couldn't take the pressure, "And if you say this [being silent under pressure] has never happened to you, well, there are two reasons why you can say that: One, you've never taken a stand for anything and,

Two, you avoid conflict at all costs." If we question Peter's weakness and criticize his failure, what are we missing about grace?

3  In John 21, we catch up with Peter on a fishing trip after the resurrection. He was still in failure mode, but Jesus was about to restore him. (Have someone read John 21:15-19). Pastor Rick's first point was that boldness won't happen unless we create time for intimate fellowship with Jesus. What are some ways we can do that?

4  Point two in Peter's transformation to boldness was listening with his heart as much as his head. How do you see that in John 21, and what would it mean in your life?

5  Concentrating on God's total and complete forgiveness was Peter's third move toward boldness. How does radical forgiveness promote personal boldness?

6  Similar to the way the group was encouraged to do at the end of the video, who would like to take a small step of boldness and share with the rest of us how God stepped into your life with the simple grace of absolute forgiveness?

# GOING DEEPER

You can explore the following Bible passages behind the teaching for this session as a group (if there is time) or on your own between sessions.

**READ 1 PETER 1:4-7.**

The same Peter whose major failure we looked at in this session also wrote some amazing stuff to keep us hopeful in our own struggles and failures. He's a great example of 'it takes one to know one' as a guide for finding good mentors. Look for someone who is willing to share how they have struggled with what you struggle with and then consider what they have to share.

- Without using the word 'grace,' (this passage is filled with examples of it), what are some examples of Peter's understanding of God's grace in these verses?

- What parts of this passage are about our 'now' experience and what parts are about our 'future' hope?

- How would you use this passage to encourage someone else to lean into God's simple grace?

## READ ROMANS 5:1-5.

In the middle of building a great case for God's intimate and timeless plan of salvation for mankind, Paul pauses to break down the way God works out His will in our lives, much along the lines James used above. As we might expect, Paul includes some unique highlights of his own.

- How are the three Persons of the Trinity active in our experience with God, according to these verses?


- Faith, hope, and love frequently show up together in Paul's writing. How is each one present in our spiritual lives?


- Paul's thought process begins and ends with hope. What steps of growth does he spell out in verses 2-5?


- What is your own most current experience of this process in which God is working in your life?

# SHARING TOGETHER

Now it's time to apply what we've been thinking about in the last few minutes.

1   When Pastor Rick asked us all to close our eyes at the end of the gospel presentation, what was your response? Did you place your faith and trust in the Lord Jesus Christ for the first time? If so, please share this with someone in your group so you can celebrate this important decision.

2   What's the hardest question or obstacle between you and God's simple grace?

3   What would you like to settle or get clearer in your mind and heart about God's grace as a result of this study?

# GOING TOGETHER

During these sessions we are doing things "together": learning, thinking, growing, sharing, praying, etc. Part of meeting together is how we live when we aren't together. Here are some opportunities to clarify our shared purposes until we meet again.

1   Part of the "together" style of these sessions is an emphasis on seeking and welcoming new people into the group. Who might you invite to join us for these sessions? If someone came to mind, write their name(s) here and think about how to best contact them.

2   Also consider someone—in this group or outside it—that you can begin going deeper with in a bolder way. This might be your mom or dad, a cousin, an aunt or uncle, a roommate, a college buddy, or a neighbor. Choose someone who might be open to "doing life" with you at a deeper level and pray about that opportunity.

3   Allow everyone to answer this question: "How can we pray for you this week?" Invite everyone to share, but don't force the issue. Be sure to write prayer requests on your Prayer and Praise Report on page 135.

Close your meeting with prayer. Encourage each other to pray audibly for others in the group.

# DAILY DEVOTIONALS

## DAY 1

(Read Day 1 in *Grace Happens*)
**Read Job 23:10**

Difficulties and Dross

*But he knows the way that I take; when he has tested me, I will come forth as gold.*

### RESPOND:

Where is simple grace in this verse? How does it describe the crucible that is the Christian life for you?

## DAY 2

(Read Day 2 in *Grace Happens*)
**Read 1 Peter 3:8 (ICB)**

The Work of Grace

*Christ himself died for you. And that one death paid for your sins. He was not guilty, but he died for those who are guilty. He did this to bring you all to God. His body was killed, but he was made alive in the spirit.*

### RESPOND:

What three actions did Jesus' death accomplish according to this verse? How do you respond to this amazing grace?

# DAY 3

(Read Day 3 in *Grace Happens*)
**Read Romans 5:1**

New Peace

*Therefore, since we have been justified through faith, we have peace with God through our Lord Jesus Christ.*

## RESPOND:

Before you read this verse again, say, "God has showered simple grace on my life. Therefore ...." How do you recognize the peace you have in Christ?

# DAY 4

(Read Day 4 in *Grace Happens*)
**Read Peter 5:10a (ICB)**

Unavoidable Learning

*Yes, you will suffer for a short time. But after that, God will make everything right. He will make you strong. He will support you and keep you from falling. He is the God who gives all grace.*

## RESPOND:

Does Peter's description of your situation as "suffer for a short time" match your current outlook or does it challenge you to change your perspective on events? How?

## DAY 5

(Read Day 5 in *Grace Happens*)
**Read Romans 5:8 (ESV)**

Grace Anticipated

*But God shows his love for us in that while we were still sinners, Christ died for us.*

**RESPOND:**
Which words (maybe all) connect for you most clearly with God's simple grace?

## DAY 6

(Read Day 6 in *Grace Happens*)
**Read Corinthians 1:3 (NLT)**

Transformational Greetings

*May God our Father and the Lord Jesus Christ give you grace and peace.*

**RESPOND:**
Most of Paul's letters begin with this greeting. How would it change your relationships if you greeted everyone with grace and peace?

# DAY 7

(Read Day 7 in *Grace Happens*)
**Read Proverbs 21:21 (ICB)**

Simple Living in Grace

*A person who tries to live right and be loyal finds life, success and honor.*

**RESPOND:**
In what ways does this slice of wisdom match your daily life?

# WEEKLY MEMORY VERSE

Yes, you will suffer for a short time. But after that, God will make everything right. He will make you strong. He will support you and keep you from falling. He is the God who gives all grace.

1 Peter 5:10a (ICB)

SESSION TWO

# CONSTANT GRACE

Welcome to week two of *Grace Happens –
40 Days of Grace*. This week we are going
to add to our understanding of simple grace
with another amazing and unexpected
characteristic: God's grace is constant. I've
summarized this as the undercurrent of God's
favor toward us that motivates and sustains
us on a daily basis. It's easier to see grace as
a momentary gesture on our behalf than to
see God's continual, relentless, unstoppable,
and always there grace. Let's see together
what that looks like.

GRACE HAPPENS   40 DAYS OF GRACE

35

# COMING
# TOGETHER

During each session, we will begin with a question or brief activity designed to "put us on the same page" for the session. If someone new has joined your group this week, please take a few minutes to introduce yourselves.

1   What would be an example of someone or something being constant in your life?

2   For the benefit of those who weren't here last time (or may have a short-term memory challenge) what lasting idea from the last session has been on your mind this past week that you would be willing to mention to the rest of the group?

3 In the next two minutes how much can we as a group remember about the story of Ruth in the Old Testament?

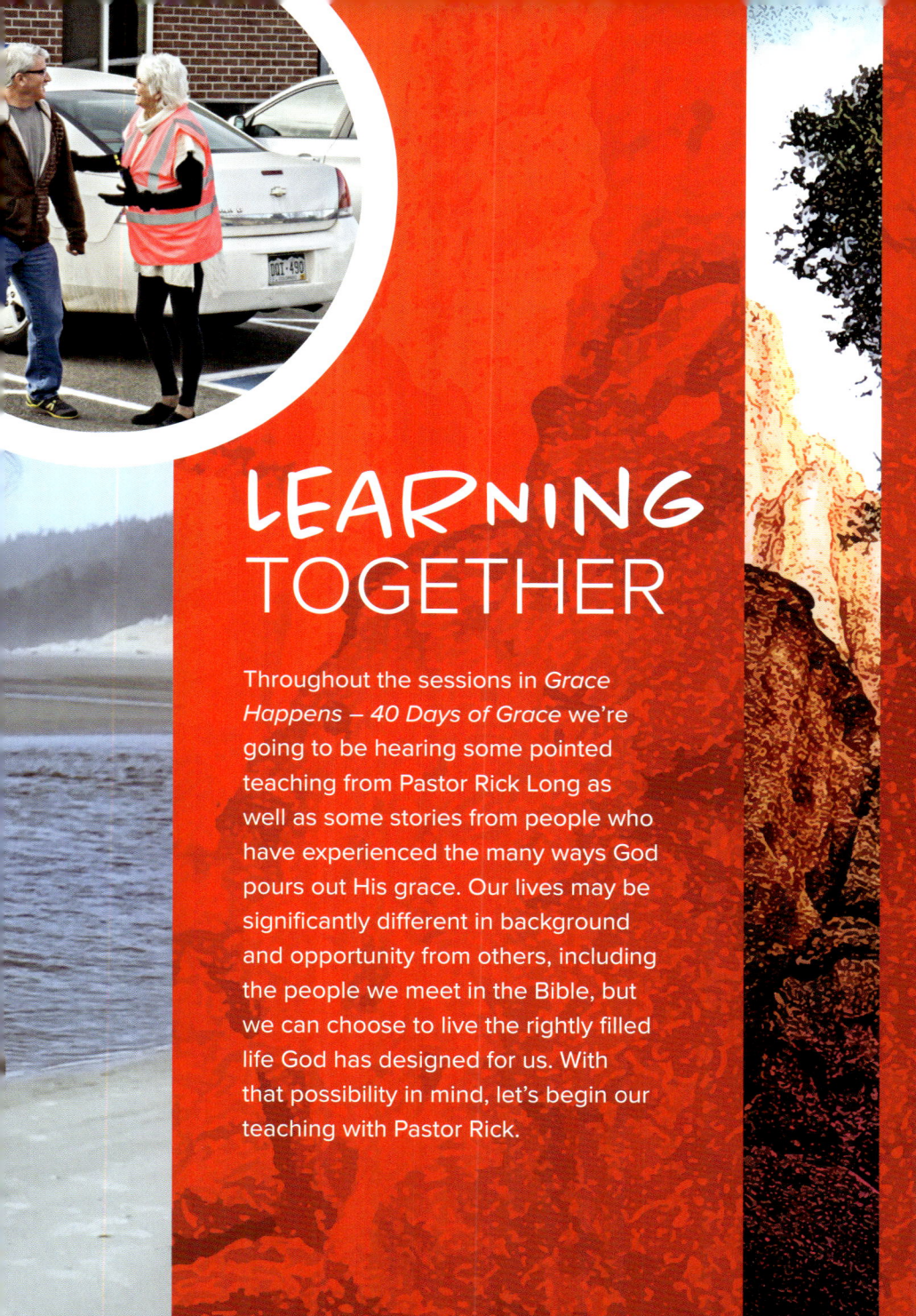

# LEARNING
# TOGETHER

Throughout the sessions in *Grace Happens – 40 Days of Grace* we're going to be hearing some pointed teaching from Pastor Rick Long as well as some stories from people who have experienced the many ways God pours out His grace. Our lives may be significantly different in background and opportunity from others, including the people we meet in the Bible, but we can choose to live the rightly filled life God has designed for us. With that possibility in mind, let's begin our teaching with Pastor Rick.

# WATCH
## THE VIDEO

## SESSION 2

Use the space provided on the next page for notes, questions and comments you want to bring up in the discussion later.

# GROWING TOGETHER

After watching the video, the following questions will help you review and expand on the teaching you just experienced. Have a volunteer read the questions and facilitate the discussion among the group.

1   Let's have a few of us share what has been a wake-up call from God for us like some in the live audience just shared?

2   Based on Pastor Rick's comments, how would you describe the characteristics of God's constant grace? What would be an example of constant grace from your own life?

3   At one point, Pastor Rick said, "In the book of Ruth, we see this (constant grace) demonstrated so clearly, the love that Ruth, the Moabite woman, had for her mother-in-law Naomi. The love Boaz had for Ruth. The kinsman-redeemer's commitment to God. And God's love for a Moabite woman and his desire to preserve the

lineage of Israel through her, not to mention bring the Messiah Jesus into the world." How does God's involvement in your life, as He was in Ruth's, become a motivating factor in the decisions and choices you make?

4   Pastor Rick noted seven different ways in which we pass on constant grace to others that we have experienced from God. As you read through this list, discuss what they mean and suggest specific ways each of these constant grace hand-offs could be made. You give constant grace to others by:

a. Your language and tone.
b. Your actions and selfless service.
c. Your ability to forgive and live at peace with others.
d. Your humility.
e. Your holy life.
f.  Your mentorship.
g. Your biblical convictions.

5   All of the above are building blocks of a legacy you are leaving. At this point, what kind of legacy are you leaving?

6   In light of God's constant grace in your life, in what areas above are you motivated to do better?

7   In Pastor Rick's closing words he said, "Salvation is the moment that we believe, but constant grace is our everyday walk. The Bible says, 'Work out your salvation.' It doesn't say work for. And each day we are working out that salvation. We are walking in the purposes of God, learning what it means to experience his grace." How do you find these words of grace motivating in your life?

# GOING
# DEEPER

You can explore the following Bible passages behind the teaching for this session as a group (if there is time) or on your own between sessions.

## READ EPHESIANS 2:6-10

There are not too many things we can think of that are more persistent or constant than death. Paul uses this fact to remind us that without Christ we are dead in our sins (Ephesians 2:1). This set up the amazing revelation that God's constant grace is greater even than death and can bring us to new life.

- How does the picture of God's constant grace come through in these verses even though that term isn't used?

- Make a list of everything God does in these verses. What do we do?

- How might God, preparing good works for us to do, (v. 10) include leaving a legacy of grace for others?

# READ 2 CORINTHIANS 4:7-18

Grace shines most brightly in places where grace seems unlikely. In difficult and overwhelming situations, Paul shows us, grace handles adversity with persistence.

- Why are we called "jars of clay" (v. 7)?

- What four kinds of experiences does Paul mention in verses 8-9? How does constant grace manage to stay constant?

- Why doesn't Paul "lose heart" (v. 16) in the face of difficulties?

- What is Paul talking about in the phrase "eternal weight of glory" (v. 17)?

# SHARING
# TOGETHER

Now it's time to apply what we've been thinking about in the last few minutes.

1   Which of the three people in the story of Ruth (Naomi, Ruth, and Boaz) do you personally identify with the most? Why?

2   At this point in your experience with Christ, how have you come to understand the constant nature of God's grace?

# GOING
# TOGETHER

During these sessions we are doing things "together": learning, thinking, growing, sharing, praying, etc. Part of meeting together is how we live when we aren't together. Here are some opportunities to clarify our shared purposes until we meet again.

1   What's one idea from this session you plan to talk about with someone beyond this group this week? Why?

2   Take a look at the Circles of Life diagram on page 133 and write the names of two or three people you know who need to experience a new or deeper relationship with Christ. Commit to praying for God's guidance and an opportunity to share with each of them.

3   Allow everyone to answer this question: "How can we pray for you this week?" Allow enough time for everyone who wants to share. Be sure to write prayer requests on your Prayer and Praise Report on page 135.

Close your meeting with prayer. Encourage each other to pray audibly for others in the group.

# DAILY DEVOTIONALS

## DAY 8

(Read Day 8 in *Grace Happens*)
**Read 2 Corinthians 4:16 (MSG)**

Unfolding Grace

*So we're not giving up. How could we! Even though on the outside it often looks like things are falling apart on us, on the inside, where God is making new life, not a day goes by without his unfolding grace.*

**RESPOND:**
How have you experienced God's "unfolding grace" in your life?

## DAY 9

(Read Day 9 in *Grace Happens*)
**Read 2 Corinthians 3:17-18 (LB)**

Grace in Sight

*The Lord is the Spirit who gives them life, and where he is there is freedom from trying to be saved by keeping the laws of God. But we Christians have no veil over our faces; we can be mirrors that brightly reflect the glory of the Lord. And as the Spirit of the Lord works within us, we become more and more like him.*

**RESPOND:**
Why is the veil absent in lives? What is the result of God's Spirit working in us?

# DAY 10

(Read Day 10 in *Grace Happens*)
**Read Hebrews 4:16 (TEV)**

The Bold Approach

*Let us have confidence, then, and approach God's throne, where there is grace. There we will receive mercy and find grace to help us just when we need it.*

**RESPOND:**
How does God's constant grace encourage your confidence?

# DAY 11

(Read Day 11 in *Grace Happens*)
**Read Ruth 1:16-17 (LB)**

The Grace of Commitment

*But Ruth replied, "Don't make me leave you, for I want to go wherever you go and to live wherever you live; your people shall be my people, and your God shall be my God; I want to die where you die and be buried there. May the Lord do terrible things to me if I allow anything but death to separate us."*

**RESPOND:**
How does God's constant grace draw you to Him?

# DAY 12

(Read Day 12 in *Grace Happens*)
**Read Ephesians 4:15 (LB)**

Christlikeness

*Instead, we will lovingly follow the truth at all times—speaking truly, dealing truly, living truly—and so become more and more in every way like Christ who is the Head of his body, the Church.*

**RESPOND:**
In what ways do you long to be more like Christ?

# DAY 13

(Read Day 13 in *Grace Happens*)
**Read Psalm 144:12b (NLT)**

The Beauty of Character

*"May our daughters be like graceful pillars, carved to beautify a palace."*

**RESPOND:**
Any parent appreciates the heartfelt blessings of others. How do you pray for and express your hopes for the children of others?

# DAY 14

(Read Day 14 in *Grace Happens*)
**Read Proverbs 10:7 (NIV)**

Good Remembrances

*"The memory of the righteous will be a blessing..."*

**RESPOND:**
Think of a saint or two whose memory is sweet to you, and tell someone else about them today, passing on the blessing of their lives.

# WEEKLY MEMORY VERSE

Let us have confidence, then, and approach God's throne, where there is grace. There we will receive mercy and find grace to help us just when we need it.

Hebrews 4:16 (TEV)

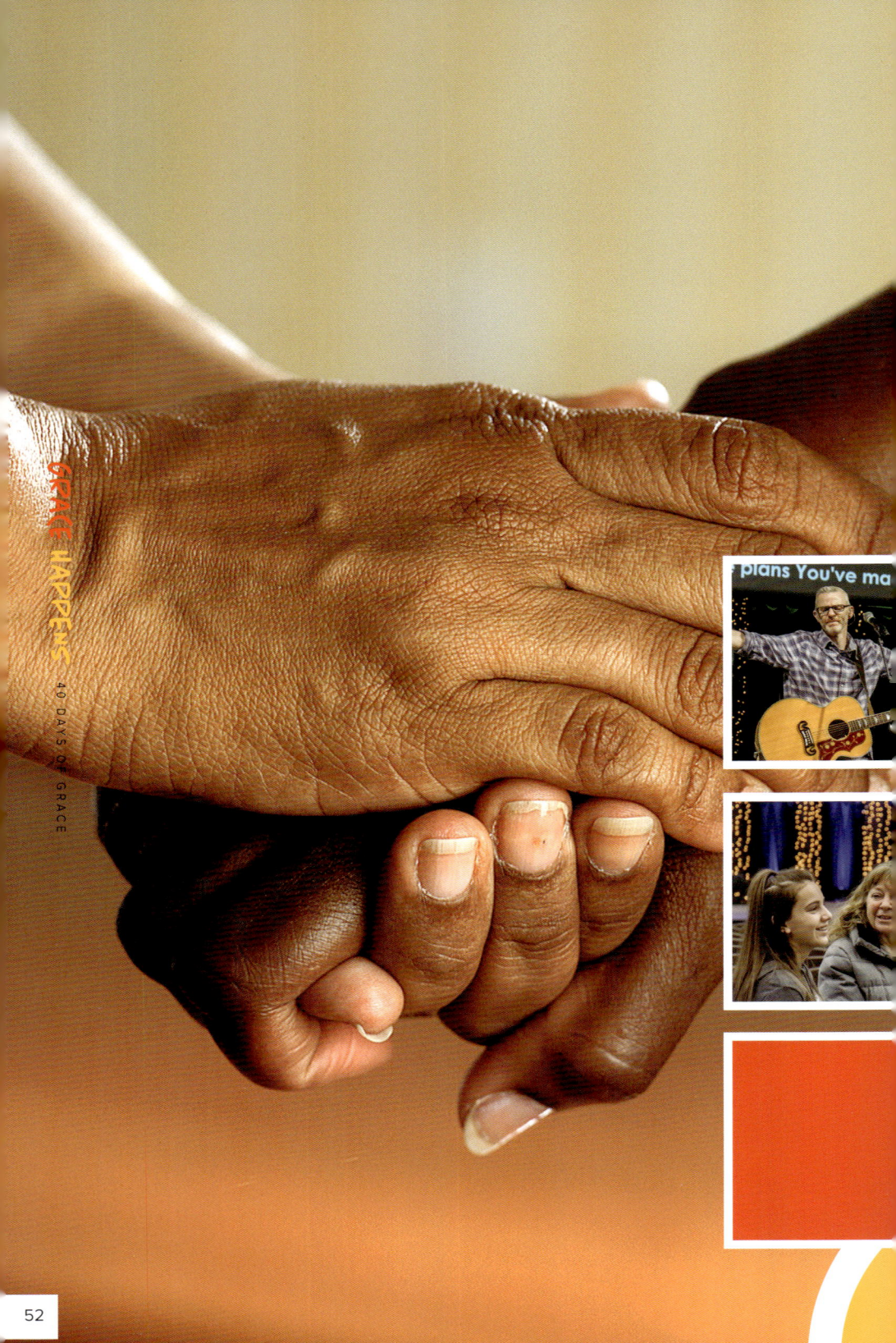

plans You've ma

## SESSION THREE

# COMFORTING GRACE

As we begin this third session of *Grace Happens – 40 Days of Grace* we move toward that expression of God's grace that moves toward us when we are helpless, hopeless, and hurting. This is the grace that comes looking for us in life's storms, the grace that finds us. It's the grace that happens when we need it even more than we know. Interestingly, that grace often comes to us through others.

# COMING
# TOGETHER

During each session, we will begin with a question or brief activity designed to "put us on the same page" for the session.

1   What are the two or three most desirable traits of the church where you are a member?

2   Describe how you personally have benefitted from one of those traits.

3   In your experience, what does it take to offer comfort to someone?

# LEARNING TOGETHER

Throughout the sessions in *Grace Happens – 40 Days of Grace* we're going to be hearing some pointed teaching from Pastor Rick Long as well as some stories from people who have experienced the many ways God pours out His grace. As you watch the teaching, fill in the acrostic on page 59, noting "the" Bible passages that are used.

# WATCH
## THE VIDEO

GRACE
HAPPENS

SESSION 1 - SESSION 2 - SESSION 3 - SESSION 4 - SESSION 5 - SESSION 6

## SESSION 3

Use the space provided on the next page for notes,
questions and comments you want to bring up in
the discussion later.

C
O
M
F
O
R
T

EXIT

# GROWING
# TOGETHER

After watching the video, the following questions will help you review and expand on the teaching you just experienced. Have a volunteer read the questions and facilitate the discussion among the group.

1   What makes a "grace centered" church and how does it differ from others?

2   The "C" in Comfort stands for "Communicate the gospel faithfully to those lost in sin." Whose responsibility is this and how do we carry it out if we're not the preacher?

3   "Offer compassionate care to anyone in need" and "Mourn

emphatically with hope for the broken-hearted" represent the "O" and the "M" in Comfort. How do these two qualities shape the way we treat others as we carry out the "C" above?

4   How do "Forget the past and focus on the future" and "Overlook offenses, our battle is not with people," the "F" and "O" in Comfort, describe our own response to the gospel as well as our view of others and their needs?

5   Alongside communicating the gospel, how does the "R" in Comfort, "Reach out to someone 'new' every weekend ... New to me," include other aspects of a healthy life as the church?

6   The "T" in Comfort stands for "Trade my desires for God's purposes" and expresses the over-all attitude of an authentic follower of Jesus. How would you put this in your own words? Include some specific examples.

7   Which of the underlying verses and principles under COMFORT that Pastor Rick used had the most compelling effect on you?

# GOING
# DEEPER

You can explore the following Bible passages behind the teaching for this session as a group (if there is time) or on your own between sessions.

## READ GALATIANS 5:13-15

Paul's letter to this church is a call to all of us not to settle for any guidelines other than Christ Himself; not any form of legalism or the encouragement to follow our own desires rather than God's Word.

- Give some examples of how freedom without guidelines or purpose can quickly become slavery.

- How does loving our neighbor as ourselves out of obedience to God actually meet the most important purposes of life?

- In your own life, how has the freedom given to you by God's grace been a comfort while living in the world?

## READ LUKE 6:27-36

These words from Jesus sound radical in a culture that glorifies personal autonomy and easy offenses. Christ never promised that following Him would give us a life full of fairness. The grace of God is not fair—and remembering that God hasn't treated us as we deserved should affect every decision we make in life.

- Which phrase in these verses gives you the hardest immediate challenge?

- In what ways has the church or you been involved in giving help and comfort to those who had no way to repay?

- What might we actually do for those who hate us? How do we go about passing on the grace we have received to others who have rejected Christ or us?

# SHARING
## TOGETHER

Now it's time to apply what we've been thinking about in the last few minutes. God's comforting grace must be part of our overall understanding of grace or we are liable to make His grace something else.

1  How did you reach out to someone new to you this past weekend? What would it take to do better next weekend?

2  Describe a personal desire that you are not sure is part of God's purpose, but you are willing to place before Him for confirmation or setting aside?

3  When you've had to give up a desire or objective in the past, how have you discovered God's comforting grace in providing something even better?

# GOING
# TOGETHER

During these sessions we are doing things "together": learning, thinking, growing, sharing, praying, etc. Part of meeting together is how we live when we aren't together. Here are some opportunities to clarify our shared purposes until we meet again.

1   What are some ways in which we could work together to supply God's comforting grace to others that we are not doing right now?

2   Allow everyone to answer this question: "How can we pray for you this week?" Invite everyone to share, but don't force the issue. Be sure to write prayer requests on your Prayer and Praise Report on page 135.

Close your meeting with prayer. Encourage each other to pray audibly for others in the group.

# DAILY DEVOTIONALS

## DAY 15

(Read Day 15 in *Grace Happens*)
**Read John 13:34-35 (ICB)**

Authentication

*I give you a new command: Love each other. You must love each other as I have loved you. All people will know that you are my followers if you love each other.*

**RESPOND:**
When have you seen the love between Christians make a difference for the watching world?

## DAY 16

(Read Day 16 in *Grace Happens*)
**Read 2 Timothy 1:9-10 (NIV)**

Timeless Grace

*He has saved us and called us to a holy life—not because of anything we have done but because of his own purpose and grace. This grace was given us in Christ Jesus before the beginning of time, but it has now been revealed through the appearing of our Savior, Christ Jesus, who has destroyed death and has brought life and immortality to light through the gospel.*

**RESPOND:**
How does it affect you to know that God's comforting grace wasn't offered to you on a whim or as an afterthought?

# DAY 17

(Read Day 17 in *Grace Happens*)
**Read Philippians 3:13-14 (ICB)**

Reaching for It

*Brothers, I know that I have not yet reached that goal. But there is one thing I always do: I forget the things that are past. I try as hard as I can to reach the goal that is before me. I keep trying to reach the goal and get the prize. That prize is mine because God called me through Christ to the life above.*

**RESPOND:**
What is the goal or prize Paul is talking about here? How are you reaching for it today?

# DAY 18

(Read Day 18 in *Grace Happens*)
**Read Ephesians 1:11-12 (MSG)**

Gracious Observation

*It's in Christ that we find out who we are and what we are living for. Long before we first heard of Christ and got our hopes up, he had his eye on us, had designs on us for glorious living, part of the overall purpose he is working out in everything and everyone.*

**RESPOND:**
How does the fact that God is watching over you for His purposes bring you comfort today?

# DAY 19

(Read Day 19 in *Grace Happens*)
**Read Matthew 5:4 (NIV)**

The Way to Comfort

*Blessed are those who mourn, for they will be comforted.*

**RESPOND:**
When or where have you observed that mourning and mourning with those who are mourning makes way for God's comforting grace?

# DAY 20

(Read Day 20 in *Grace Happens*)
**Read Proverbs 12:1 (ICB)**

Comforting Correction

*Anyone who loves learning accepts being corrected. But a person who hates being corrected is stupid.*

**RESPOND:**
What does helpful and wise correction tell you about the attitude toward you of the one correcting?

# DAY 21

(Read Day 21 in *Grace Happens*)
**Read Romans 5:20 (NIV)**

Matching Moves

*The law was added so that the trespass might increase. But where sin increased, grace increased all the more . . ."*

**RESPOND:**
In what ways have you experienced God's convicting grace in the face of sin this week?

## WEEKLY MEMORY VERSE

He has saved us and called us to a holy life—not because of anything we have done but because of his own purpose and grace. This grace was given us in Christ Jesus before the beginning of time, but it has now been revealed through the appearing of our Savior, Christ Jesus, who has destroyed death and has brought life and immortality to light through the gospel.

2 Timothy 1:9-10 (NIV)

SESSION FOUR

# FEARLESS GRACE

Welcome to session four of *Grace Happens – 40 Days of Grace*! For the rest of our sessions, we are going to see grace in action. Coming off our last session on comforting grace, it may seem at first a little jolt to talk about fearless grace, but we have to remember that God's grace is not only given to us but it also wants to affect the world through us. It might come as a surprise to discover that grace is fearless!

# COMING TOGETHER

Open your time with prayer that the lessons of grace will have lasting impact in the group and beyond it. As we have been doing each week, we begin with a question or brief activity designed to "put us on the same page" for the session.

1   Who has an observation from this past few days of seeing God's grace in action?

2   One of the things people have to get used to when they are reading the Bible is all the strange names. Who's your candidate for Most Unusual Name in the Bible?

3   What does it mean to act fearlessly? When have you seen that happen recently?

# LEARNING
# TOGETHER

Throughout the sessions in *Grace Happens – 40 Days of Grace* we're going to be hearing some pointed teaching from Pastor Rick Long as well as some stories from people who have experienced the many ways God pours out His grace.

# WATCH
## THE VIDEO

## SESSION 4

Use the space provided on the next page for notes,
questions and comments you want to bring up in
the discussion later.

# GROWING
# TOGETHER

After watching the video, the following questions will help us review and expand on the teaching we just experienced. Have a volunteer read the questions and facilitate the discussion among the group.

1   Mephibosheth is one of those Bible names we don't want to say three times quickly! From Pastor Rick's comments on his life, what impression do you have about Mephibosheth?

2   Pastor Rick mentioned five different causes for fear in Mephibosheth's life. How many can we remember? What similar causes create fear in us?

3  If someone like Mephibosheth visited our small group what clues would we look for that might help us see his needs? How are people crippled in other ways than just physically?

4  What's surprising about David's graciousness toward the family of Saul? According to 1 Samuel 20:13-17, what promise was David keeping in treating Mephibosheth kindly?

5  At the point in the Bible when we meet Mephibosheth, we think of David as a fearless leader and Mephibosheth not nearly so fearless. But how did grace allow both David and Mephibosheth to act fearlessly in new ways?

6  Pastor Rick outlined five factors in fearless grace from Romans 8. After each one, brainstorm possible results or purposes based on that grace-strengthening factor:

   a. Understand there is no eternal condemnation, so there should be no personal condemnation (vv. 1-5).

   b. Our bodies will die, but our souls will live on forever (vv. 11-14).

   c. We are God's children, not His puppets (vv. 15-27).

   d. Our problem becomes God's plan to produce our greatest potential (vv. 28-37).

   e. Knowing that we cannot be separated from God for any reason, not any reason at all (vv. 38-39).

# GOING DEEPER

You can explore the following Bible passages behind the teaching for this session as a group (if there is time) or on your own between sessions.

## READ ROMANS 8:31-39

In this powerful passage in Paul's writing, he takes the reality of God's love to another level, inviting us to imagine all the things that might inspire fear in us but in fact are simply reminders that absolutely nothing can separate us from the love of Christ.

- Why should we feel confident that God is not against us or condemning us?

- What specific powers, tragedies, or hardships are unable to separate us from the love of Christ?

- What situations or thoughts are most likely to make you feel you are separated from God's love? How does this passage address those fears?

**Read 2 Samuel 9:1-13**

As you read through the brief account of David's dealings with Mephibosheth, keep in mind both the people in your past who have practiced grace toward you that made a difference and listen for God's Spirit bringing people to mind toward whom you can practice fearless grace.

- What were the differences between how Ziba and Mephibosheth saw him and how David saw Mephibosheth? Why did that matter?

- What "crippled" people have had the biggest impact in your life?

- In what specific ways are you seeking to reach out in grace to those who are "crippled" in some way in this life?

# SHARING TOGETHER

Now it's time to apply what we've been thinking about in the last few minutes.

1   Thinking of David's example and the stories we heard from the panel, what's the difference between being gracious when people and situations come to us and tracking down people in order to be gracious to them?

2   In closing, Pastor Rick referred to the final verses of Romans 8 and said, "I don't know what you've done, who you've done it with, how many times you've done it, where you've done it or whether you'll do it again, but I know if you are a Christian born into the family of God, nothing absolutely nothing can separate you from God's love." How does confidence in Christ and His love inspire fearlessness in you?

# *GOING*
# TOGETHER

During these sessions we are doing things "together": learning, thinking, growing, sharing, praying, etc. Part of meeting together is how we live when we aren't together. Here are some opportunities to clarify our shared purposes until we meet again.

1   What aspects of fearless grace are you taking away from this study to practice in your life? Do you need to admit more of the Mephibosheth in you or practice more of the David in you?

2   Allow everyone to answer this question: "How can we pray for you this week?" Invite everyone to share, but don't force the issue. Be sure to write prayer requests on your Prayer and Praise Report on page 135.

Close your meeting with prayer. Encourage each other to pray audibly for others in the group.

# DAILY
# DEVOTIONALS

## DAY 22

(Read Day 22 in *Grace Happens*)
**Read 1 John 4:18 (NIV2011)**

Fearless Love

*There is no fear in love. But perfect love drives out fear, because fear has to do with punishment. The one who fears is not made perfect in love.*

### RESPOND:

List some of the ways God's grace and His love have worked together to change you? Take time to thank Him for that amazing work.

## DAY 23

(Read Day 23 in *Grace Happens*)
**Read 2 Timothy 1:7 (NIV2011)**

The Spirit's By-products

*For the Spirit God gave us does not make us timid, but gives us power, love and self-discipline.*

### RESPOND:

Whish of the three bi-products of the Spirit do you need most today? Take a moment to ask Him for it.

# DAY 24

(Read Day 24 in *Grace Happens*)
**Read Romans 8:1-2 (NLT)**

No Condemnation!

*So now there is no condemnation for those who belong to Christ Jesus. And because you belong to him, the power of the life-giving Spirit has freed you from the power of sin that leads to death.*

**RESPOND:**
Where in your life right now do you need to fearlessly practice more of this freedom you have in Christ?

# DAY 25

(Read Day 25 in *Grace Happens*)
**Read Romans 3:23 (NIV)**

Equal Condition Reality

*For all have sinned and fall short of the glory of God ...*

**RESPOND:**
How does the truth that we're all in the same boat as sinners free you up to experience and express God's fearless grace in your life?

# DAY 26

(Read Day 26 in *Grace Happens*)
**Read Romans 8:38-39 (NLT)**

Inseparable!

*And I am convinced that nothing can ever separate us from God's love. Neither death nor life, neither angels nor demons, neither our fears for today nor our worries about tomorrow—not even the powers of hell can separate us from God's love. No power in the sky above or in the earth below—indeed, nothing in all creation will ever be able to separate us from the love of God that is revealed in Christ Jesus our Lord.*

**RESPOND:**
Who could you tell today how glad you are that nothing can separate them from the love of God expressed in Christ Jesus?

# DAY 27

(Read Day 27 in *Grace Happens*)
**Read Romans 8:37 (NASB)**

Winners and Then Some

*But in all these things we overwhelmingly conquer through Him who loved us.*

**RESPOND:**
What are some areas in your life where fearless grace need to overwhelmingly conquer? Who's praying with you about that?

# DAY 28

(Read Day 28 in *Grace Happens*)
**Read 2 Corinthians 12:9-10 (ICB)**

The Real Source

*"But the Lord said to me, 'My grace is enough for you. When you are weak, then my power is made perfect in you.' So I am very happy to brag about my weaknesses. Then Christ's power can live in me. So I am happy when I have weaknesses, insults, hard times, sufferings, and all kinds of troubles. All these things are for Christ. And I am happy, because when I am weak, then I am truly strong."*

**RESPOND:**

How have you personally discovered that God's grace sometimes offers a way out and sometimes offers a way through?

# WEEKLY MEMORY VERSE

For God has not given us a spirit of fear and timidity, but of power, love, and self-discipline.

2 Timothy 1:7 (NLT)

GRACE HAPPENS

# SELFLESS GRACE

Someone once said that the real test of owning something is the capacity to give it away. If you can't give it away, it owns you, not the other way around. If this is true of our possessions, could it be true of our faith? Could it be true of grace?

What if things really aren't "ours" until we give them away? Until we try to explain what we believe or express it through grace, there's room for lots of doubt about the reality of our faith. In this session we will look at the importance of deliberately making room for selfless grace that doesn't seek to be recognized or rewarded.

# COMING
# TOGETHER

Open with prayer. Let's begin with a question or brief activity designed to "put us on the same page" for the session.

1   As we arrive at this fifth session of *Grace Happens – 40 Days of Grace,* we may all be thinking about grace more than we have in a long time. Based on your new understandings, what are some ways you would finish the statement: *Grace Happens* when …

2   We're born selfish; we have to learn selflessness. What's one of your earliest remembered lessons in selflessness?

# LEARNING TOGETHER

Throughout these sessions in *Grace Happens – 40 Days of Grace*, we've been hearing some pointed teaching from Pastor Rick Long as well as some stories from people who have experienced the many ways God pours out His grace.

# WATCH
## THE VIDEO

GRACE HAPPENS

SESSION 1 - SESSION 2 - SESSION 3 - SESSION 4 - SESSION 5 - SESSION 6

## SESSION 5

Use the space provided on the next page for notes,
questions and comments you want to bring up in
the discussion later.

# GROWING
## TOGETHER

After watching the video, the following questions will help you review and expand on the teaching you just experienced. Have a volunteer read the questions and facilitate the discussion among the group.

1   "Selfless people don't think less of themselves they think of themselves … less." How would you explain the truth of this quote?

2   Pastor Rick made the point that in the great passage on Jesus' selflessness in Philippians 2:5-11, the two key words to selflessness are think and act. How did he combine this truth with the Great Commandment and our vertical and horizontal relationships?

3  Let's talk about the significance of each of the four examples of selflessness that we can find Jesus teaching in Matthew 5. Read each of these and comment on them as a guide for selfless living:

a. Jesus taught us about selfless grace in his stops not (just) his steps.

b. Jesus taught us selflessness through eight principles of happiness or blessing, which are all selfless.

c. Jesus taught us that selfless people shine the light of the gospel on their communities.

d. Jesus taught us to love our enemies, not just our friends.

4  Have someone read Matthew 5:3-11 and discuss how each of the Beatitudes involves an action of selflessness.

5  What does the fact mean for you that all these are demonstrated and commanded by Jesus rather than suggestions He made? Do we treat them as optional or as opportunities to gratefully obey the One who loves us and died for us?

6  How were you impacted by the stories of selflessness shared by the panel?

7  Why is the order important in the names represented by J.O.Y., as Pastor Rick explained?

*Jesus Others Yourself*

*Puts Jesus's before others yourself!*

# GOING
# DEEPER

You can explore the following Bible passages behind the teaching for this session as a group (if there is time) or on your own between sessions.

## READ PHILIPPIANS 2:5-11

Once we understand the Jesus is our Savior and Lord, the lesson we work out for the rest of our lives is that Jesus is also our model for living. He accepted the same limitations that the rest of us as humans live with, and He showed us how to depend daily on the Holy Spirit to accomplish all of God's purposes.

- How did Jesus demonstrate selflessness in the whole process of saving us?

- What does it mean that Jesus "emptied" Himself?

- How does Jesus' humility challenge your own tendency toward self-centeredness?

## READ PHILIPPIANS 4:4-9

Among the most recognized words of Paul, these thoughts that begin with "Rejoice in the Lord always. I will say it again, rejoice" capture the bottom line of selfless living. And a lot of it has to do with the choices we make about what we will think about.

- What does rejoicing in the Lord always really look like in someone's life?

- How did Paul tell the Philippian believers to treat each other?

- List the various things we are supposed to think about and discuss how this kind of thinking changes us and affects our experience of joy.

# SHARING
# TOGETHER

Now it's time to apply what we've been thinking about in the last few minutes.

1  In the final moment of his teaching, Pastor Rick instructed us to pray for several things:

   a. Pray for forgiveness... the need to give it and the need to ask for it.

   b. Pray for the person who hurt you, that God will bless them.

   c. Then pray for an opportunity to reach out and attempt to heal the broken relationship.

What were some of your thoughts as he talked about that practice of selflessness?

2  On a scale of 1 to 10, with 1 being very low and 10 being very high, what number would you give the level of joy in your life right now? What have you learned in this session that could significantly move that number higher?

# GOING
# TOGETHER

During these sessions we are doing things "together": learning, thinking, growing, sharing, praying, etc. Part of meeting together is how we live when we aren't together. Here are some opportunities to clarify our shared purposes until we meet again.

1   Make a note of one or two people here that you need to contact this next week with a salute for how your life has benefited from their selfless commitment to the gospel.

2   Allow everyone to answer this question: "How can we pray for you this week?" Invite everyone to share, but don't force the issue. Be sure to write prayer requests on your Prayer and Praise Report on page 135.

Close your meeting with prayer. Encourage each other to pray audibly for others in the group.

# DAILY
## DEVOTIONALS

## DAY 29

(Read Day 29 in *Grace Happens*)
**Read Philippians 3:7-11 (ICB)**

New Set of Values

*At one time all these things were important to me. But now I think those things are worth nothing because of Christ. Not only those things, but I think that all things are worth nothing compared with the greatness of knowing Christ Jesus my Lord.*

**RESPOND:**
How has knowing Jesus made a difference in what you really value?

## DAY 30

(Read Day 30 in *Grace Happens*)
**Read Philippians 2:17-18 (GW)**

Joyful Outpouring

*My life is being poured out as a part of the sacrifice and service {I offer to God} for your faith. Yet, I am filled with joy, and I share that joy with all of you. For this same reason you also should be filled with joy and share that joy with me.*

**RESPOND:**
As you picture Paul's life being "poured out" what would that mean in your own life?

# DAY 31

(Read Day 31 in *Grace Happens*)
**Read Philippians 2:13-14 (GW)**

Internal Motivation

*It is God who produces in you the desires and actions that please him. Do everything without complaining or arguing.*

**RESPOND:**
How are you recognizing God at work in you to motivate actions that fit His purposes?

# DAY 32

(Read Day 32 in *Grace Happens*)
**Read Philippians 2:4 (NLT)**

Broader Interests

*Don't look out only for your own interests, but take an interest in others, too.*

**RESPOND:**
Think of two or three examples of situations right now where you are looking out for the interests of others as much or more than for your own?

# DAY 33

(Read Day 33 in *Grace Happens*)
**Read Philippians 4:7 (NLT)**

Grace

*Then you will experience God's peace, which exceeds anything we can understand. His peace will guard your hearts and minds as you live in Christ Jesus.*

**RESPOND:**
The verses before this one spell out a rejoicing mindset. How does persistent joy lead to peace?

# DAY 34

(Read Day 34 in *Grace Happens*)
**Read Matthew 5:1**

Significant Stop

*One day as he saw the crowds gathering, Jesus went up on the mountainside and sat down. His disciples gathered around him,*

**RESPOND:**
What have you discovered about the relationship between hurry and grace? When might it be good to slow down in your life in order to practice more grace?

## DAY 35

(Read Day 35 in *Grace Happens*)
**Read Deuteronomy 6:6-9 (NLT)**

Parental Grace

*And you must commit yourselves wholeheartedly to these commands that I am giving you today. Repeat them again and again to your children. Talk about them when you are at home and when you are on the road, when you are going to bed and when you are getting up. Tie them to your hands and wear them on your forehead as reminders. Write them on the doorposts of your house and on your gates.*

**RESPOND:**
What thoughts and actions that convey grace toward your children can you find in these verses?

## WEEKLY MEMORY VERSE

My life is being poured out as a part of the sacrifice and service {I offer to God} for your faith. Yet, I am filled with joy, and I share that joy with all of you. For this same reason you also should be filled with joy and share that joy with me.

Philippians 2:17-18 (GW)

SESSION SIX

# DARING GRACE

Welcome to our sixth and final session of *Grace Happens – 40 Days of Grace*. Pastor Rick has said that daring grace is an outlook which suddenly inspires unexpected boldness to change the world, starting with the person right in front of you. We're going to be talking about taking a chance as an act of obedience to God and trust in Him. This is the view of grace that takes us beyond these sessions and can make a huge difference in our families, our church, our workplace and the world.

# COMING TOGETHER

Open the meeting with prayer. As in each session, we will begin with a question or brief activity designed to "put us on the same page" for the session.

1   What's the silliest or craziest thing you've done because a friend smiled and said, "I dare you"?

2   A year from now, what do you think you will remember about these six weeks we've spent together?

3   Most of us can look back and realize that along the way, people have taken a chance with us on a team, or at work, and entrusted us with a role we hadn't really proven we could do. What was one of those for you and how did it turn out?

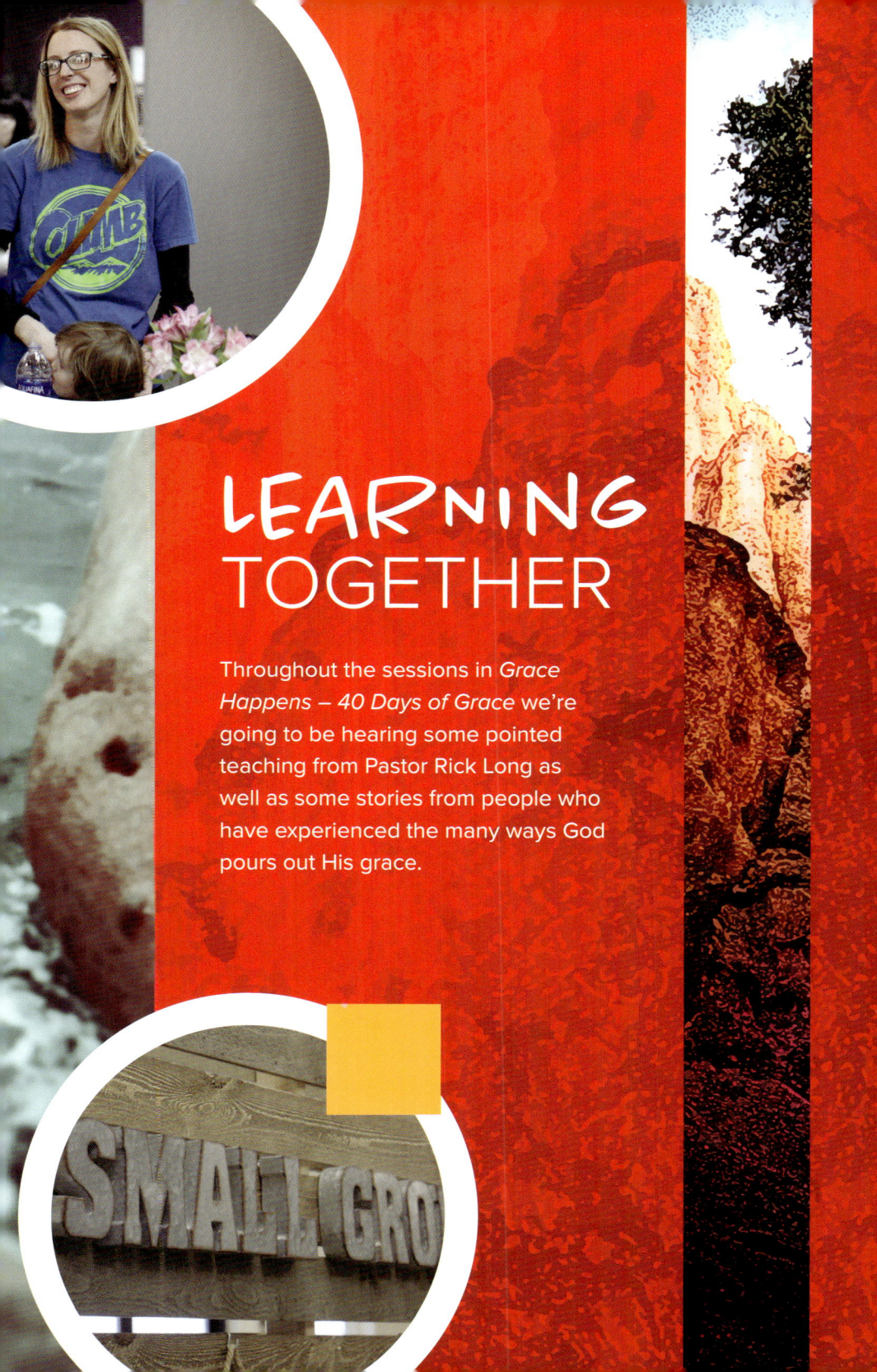

# LEARNING TOGETHER

Throughout the sessions in *Grace Happens – 40 Days of Grace* we're going to be hearing some pointed teaching from Pastor Rick Long as well as some stories from people who have experienced the many ways God pours out His grace.

# WATCH
## THE VIDEO

## SESSION 6

Use the space provided on the next page for notes, questions and comments you want to bring up in the discussion later.

# GROWING
# TOGETHER

After watching the video, the following questions will help you review and expand on the teaching you just experienced. Have a volunteer read the questions and facilitate the discussion among the group.

1   One of Pastor Rick's themes around this teaching was this: "God's daring grace rescued me from all my sin and gives me the strength to battle my sin nature daily."

Recently, when have you demonstrated the boldness of God's daring grace in your life?

2   What comments from the panel in response to the teaching were helpful for you, particularly as they dared to speak about their experience with Christ?

3  Pastor Rick quickly shared an acrostic that can be helpful in communicating the gospel to others. He called it GOTCHA GRACE:

a.  **G**od's law was simply a spiritual mirror to reveal our sin. We're all sinners.

b.  **O**ur sins separate us from God. There's nothing that we can do to get rid of them.

c.  **T**urning from all of my sin is impossible.

d.  **C**hrist fulfilled the law completely when He came into the world and lived a perfect life. Then He died on the cross and He conquered death and hell.

e.  **H**e rose from the dead.

f.  **A**nyone who believes receives the gift of salvation.

Now, that's a Gotcha Grace.

How would you go about making this message personal in your life as you share it?

4  Let's go through those seven points again and brainstorm at least one Bible verse for each one.

5  What illustrations, principles, or points have you discovered in your own experiences that help you share the gospel with others?

6  Where or when have you watched someone share the gospel in a bold way that thrilled you?

# GOING
# DEEPER

You can explore the following Bible passages behind the teaching for this session as a group (if there is time) or on your own between sessions.

## READ ROMANS 7:21—8:4

This passage comes in the middle of Paul's great testimony of sanctification. He was opening up his heart and being spiritually transparent to the Romans (and us) so that there would be no mistaking the fact that we are saved but we still struggle.

• What words does Paul use to describe the two sides of the fight inside?

• What is his hope of escape when he feels completely overwhelmed (v. 25)?

• How does Romans 8:1 declare your own relationship with God?

• Because we can't win the struggle with sin, what did God do (8:2-4)?

## READ EPHESIANS 3:14-21

Paul practices what he preached—he prayed without ceasing. He even expected those he introduced to Jesus Christ to pray for him! This passage is a glimpse into the way Paul prayed for others and it has depth that can deepen our prayers too.

- What is Paul's first request for the Ephesians (v. 16) and what would it mean to have someone praying that way for you?

- In verse 17 he uses the term "dwell," or as the Living Bible puts it, "make himself at home." Is this prayer for salvation or for a growing spiritual life?

- Describe Paul's view of Christ's love? What are its dimensions and what are its limitations?

- How do verses 20-21 declare the main reason why we ought to be committed to prayer?

# SHARING TOGETHER

Now it's time to apply what we've been thinking about in the last few minutes.

1   What are some aspects of the grace-filled gospel that are often missing from the angry, threatening, or uncaring presentations about salvation?

2   Why is it crucial that we not just settle for the work God's grace does in us but dare to share that grace with others? (See Galatians 2:21).

3   As we bring this series to a close, talk a little about how your own understanding of God's grace has deepened.

# GOING
# TOGETHER

During these sessions we are doing things "together": learning, thinking, growing, sharing, praying, etc. Part of meeting together is how we live when we aren't together. Here are some opportunities to clarify our shared purposes until we meet again.

NOTE: If you have not already done so, you may want to add some time to talk about where the group will go next in study.

1   How can we be accountable to one another in this small group for how we're cherishing and sharing God's grace in the months to come? What would be a good question we could agree to ask and answer among ourselves that would serve to keep us on track ... Something like, "So, how the daring going?"

2   Also, as you understand your own tendencies, what do you realize will be some of the obstacles that will have to be overcome as you dare to share the good news about Jesus?

3   What you've just shared is a great way for us to pray for one another. But let me also ask again: "How can we pray for you this week?" Invite everyone to share, but don't force the issue. Be sure to write prayer requests on your Prayer and Praise Report on page 135.

Close your meeting with prayer. Encourage each other to pray audibly for others in the group.

# DAILY
# DEVOTIONALS

## DAY 36

(Read Day 36 in *Grace Happens*)
**Read Ephesians 2:8-9**

God Took the Dare

*God saved you by his grace when you believed. And you can't take credit for this; it is a gift from God. Salvation is not a reward for the good things we have done, so none of us can boast about it.*

**RESPOND:**
Pray five reasons why you are thankful for God's grace.

## DAY 37

(Read Day 37 in *Grace Happens*)
**Read 2 Corinthians 9:14-15 (NJB)**

Grace=Priceless

*And so with deep affection they will pray for you because of the extraordinary grace God has shown you. Let us thank God for his priceless gift!*

**RESPOND:**
How is grace for you the gift that keeps on giving?

# DAY 38

(Read Day 38 in *Grace Happens*)
**Read Ephesians 1:11-14 (GW)**

God Knew; God
Planned; God Dared

*God also decided ahead of time to choose us through Christ according to his plan, which makes everything work the way he intends. He planned all of this so that we who had already focused our hope on Christ would praise him and give him glory.*

## RESPOND:
Put the last six words of this passage into practice right now and offer praise and glory to God for His grace.

# DAY 39

(Read Day 39 in *Grace Happens*)
**Read Ephesians 3:18-19 (CEV)**

Limitless Love

*I pray that you and all of God's people will understand what is called wide or long or high or deep. I want you to know all about Christ's love, although it is too wonderful to be measured. Then your lives will be filled with all that God is.*

## RESPOND:
What was the last amazing discovery you made about God's love?

# DAY 40

(Read Day 40 in *Grace Happens*)
**Read Romans 8:1 (GW)**

Blank and Sealed Slate

*So those who are believers in Christ Jesus can no longer be condemned.*

**RESPOND:**
How will your life today look like someone who is no longer under condemnation?

# DAY 41

(Read Day 41 in *Grace Happens*)
**Read John 10:28 (ESV)**

Confidence-based Daring

*I give them eternal life, and they will never perish. No one can snatch them away from me.*

**RESPOND:**
Once we're under Christ's protection, what are we actually doing when we fear or avoid daring to share the gospel with others?

# DAY 42

(Read Day 42 in *Grace Happens*)
**Read Romans 1:16 (NLT)**

Dynamite

*For I am not ashamed of this Good News about Christ. It is the power of God at work, saving everyone who believes—the Jew first and also the Gentile.*

## RESPOND:

Back to Peter the failure in Session 1. We shouldn't be ashamed or afraid, but we are. How has your confidence in Christ and His grace deepened throughout this study?

# WEEKLY MEMORY VERSE

And so with deep affection they will pray for you because of the extraordinary grace God has shown you. Let us thank God for his priceless gift!

2 Corinthians 9:14-15 (NJB)

# APPENDICES

Resources to make your Small Group
experience even better!

# FAQS

### What do we do on the first night of our group?

Like a l fun things in life—have a party!  A "get to know you" coffee, dinner, or dessert is a great way to launch a new study.  You may want to review the Small Group Agreement (page 128) and share the names of a few friends you can invite to join you.  But most importantly, have fun before your study time begins.

### Where do we find new members for our group?

This can be a struggle, especially for new groups that have only a few people or for existing groups that lose a few people along the way. We encourage you to pray with your group and then brainstorm a list of people from work, church, your neighborhood, your children's school, family, the gym, and so forth.  Then have each group member invite several of the people on his or her list. If you need help with recruiting new members, contact your church office or the Small Group Director. No matter how you find members, it's vital that you stay on the lookout for new people to join your group. All groups tend to go through healthy attrition—the result of moves, releasing new leaders, ministry opportunities, and so forth—and if the group gets too small, it could be at risk of shutting down. If you and your group stay open, you'll be amazed at the people God sends your way. The next person just might become a friend for life. You never know!

### How long will this group meet?

Most groups meet weekly for at least their first six weeks, but every other week can work as well. We strongly recommend that the group

meet for the first six months on a weekly basis if at all possible. This allows for continuity, and if people miss a meeting they aren't gone for a whole month.

At the end of this study, each group member may decide if he or she wants to continue on for another study. Some groups launch relationships for years to come, and others are stepping-stones into another group experience. Either way, enjoy the journey.

**Can we do this study on our own?**

Absolutely! This may sound crazy, but one of the best ways to do this study is not with a full house but with a few friends. You may choose to gather with another couple who would enjoy some relational time (perhaps going to the movies or having a quiet dinner) and then walking through this study. Jesus will be with you even if there are only two of you (Matthew 18:20).

**What if this group is not working for us?**

You're not alone! This could be the result of a personality conflict, life stage difference, geographical distance, level of spiritual maturity, or any number of things. Relax. Pray for God's direction, and at the end of this six-week study, decide whether to continue with this group or find another. You don't typically buy the first car you look at or marry the first person you date, and the same goes with a group. However, don't bail out before the six weeks are up—God might have something to teach you. Also, don't run from conflict or prejudge people before you have given them a chance. God is still working in your life, too!

**Who is the leader?**

Most groups have an official leader. But ideally, the group will mature and members will rotate the leadership of meetings. We have discovered that healthy groups rotate hosts/leaders and homes on a regular basis. This model ensures that all members grow, give their unique contribution, and develop their gifts. This study guide and the Holy Spirit can keep things on track even when you rotate leaders. Christ has promised to be in your midst as you gather. Ultimately, God is your leader each step of the way.

**How do we handle the childcare needs in our group?**
Very carefully. Seriously, this can be a sensitive issue. We suggest that you empower the group to openly brainstorm solutions. You may try one option that works for a while and then adjust over time. One approach is for adults to meet in the living room or dining room and to share the cost of a babysitter (or two) who can watch the kids in a different part of the house. This way, parents don't have to be away from their children all evening when their children are too young to be left at home. A second option is to use one home for the kids and a second home (close by or a phone call away) for the adults. Finally, the most common solution is to decide you need to have a night to invest in your spiritual lives individually or as a couple and to make your own arrangements for childcare. No matter what decision the group makes, the best approach is to dialogue openly about both the problem and the solution.

# SMALL GROUP
# AGREEMENT

## OUR PURPOSE

To provide a predictable environment where participants experience authentic community and spiritual growth.

## OUR VALUES

### Group Attendance

To give priority to the group meeting. We will call or email if we will be late or absent. (Completing the Group Calendar will minimize this issue.)

### Safe Environment

To help create a safe place where people can be heard and feel loved. (Please, no quick answers, snap judgments, or simple fixes.)

### Respect Differences

To be gentle and gracious to fellow group members with different spiritual maturity, personal opinions, temperaments, or "imperfections." We are all works in progress.

### Confidentiality

To keep anything that is shared strictly confidential and within the group, and to avoid sharing improper information about those outside the group.

### Encouragement for Growth

To be not just takers but givers of life. We want to spiritually multiply our life by serving others with our God-given gifts.

### Shared Ownership

To remember that every member is a minister and to ensure that each attencer will share different responsibilities over time.

### Rotating Hosts/Leaders and Homes

To encourage different people to host the group in their homes and to rotate the responsibility of facilitating each meeting. See Small Group Calendar.

## OUR EXPECTATIONS

- Refreshments/mealtimes:
- Childcare:
- When we will meet (day of week):
- Where we will meet (place):
- We will begin at (time):_____and end at:_____
- We will do our best to have some or all of us attend a worship service together. Our primary worship service time will be:
- Date of this agreement:
- Date we will review this agreement again:
- Who (other than the leader) will review this agreement at the end of this study:

# SMALL GROUP
## CALENDAR

Planning and keeping a calendar help ensure the greatest participation at every meeting. At the end of each meeting, review this calendar. Be sure to include a regular rotation of host homes and leaders, and don't forget birthdays, church events, holidays, and mission/ministry projects.

| Date | Lesson | Host Home | Dessert/Meal | Leader |
|------|--------|-----------|--------------|--------|
|      |        |           |              |        |

# SPIRITUAL PARTNERS' CHECK-IN PAGE

Briefly check in each week and write down your personal plans
and progress targets for the next week (or even for the next few weeks).
This could be done (before or after the meeting) on the phone, through an
e-mail message or even in person from time to time.

My Name:

Spiritual Partner's Name:

| | Our Plan | Our Progress |
|---|---|---|
| **Week 1** | | |
| **Week 2** | | |
| **Week 3** | | |
| **Week 4** | | |
| **Week 5** | | |
| **Week 6** | | |

# MEMORY VERSE
## CARDS

**SESSION ONE**

Yes, you will suffer for a short time. But after that, God will make everything right. He will make you strong. He will support you and keep you from falling. He is the God who gives all grace. **1 Peter 5:10a (ICB)**

**SESSION TWO**

Let us have confidence, then, and approach God's throne, where there is grace. There we will receive mercy and find grace to help us just when we need it. **Hebrews 4:16 (TEV)**

**SESSION THREE**

He has saved us and called us to a holy life—not because of anything we have done but because of his own purpose and grace. This grace was given us in Christ Jesus before the beginning of time, but it has now been revealed through the appearing of our Savior, Christ Jesus, who has destroyed death and has brought life and immortality to light through the gospel.
**2 Timothy 1:9-10 (NIV)**

**SESSION FOUR**

For God has not given us a spirit of fear and timidity, but of power, love, and self-discipline. **2 Timothy 1:7 (NLT)**

**SESSION FIVE**

My life is being poured out as a part of the sacrifice and service {I offer to God} for your faith. Yet, I am filled with joy, and I share that joy with all of you. For this same reason you also should be filled with joy and share that joy with me. **Philippians 2:17-18 (GW)**

**SESSION SIX**

And so with deep affection they will pray for you because of the extraordinary grace God has shown you. Let us thank God for his priceless gift!
**2 Corinthians 9:14-15 (NJB)**

# CIRCLES
## OF LIFE

### FAMILY
(immediate or extended)

_____
_____
_____
_____

### FAMILIAR
(neighbors, kids, sports teams, school, and so forth)

_____
_____
_____
_____

### FRIENDS

_____
_____
_____
_____

### FUN
(gym, hobbies, hangouts)

_____
_____
_____
_____

### FIRM
(work)

_____
_____
_____
_____

# SMALL GROUP ROSTER

| Name | Phone Number | Email | Address |
| --- | --- | --- | --- |
| | | | |

# PRAYER AND PRAISE
# REPORT

**PRAYER REQUESTS**

**PRAISE REPORT**

_____

_____

_____

_____

_____

_____

_____

_____

_____

_____

# SMALL GROUP LEADERS

Resources to make your Small Group experience even better!

*GRACE HAPPENS*

40 DAYS OF GRACE

# HOSTING AN
## OPEN HOUSE

If you're starting a new group, try planning an "open house" before your first formal group meeting. Even if you have only two to four core members, it's a great way to break the ice and to consider prayerfully who else might be open to joining you over the next few weeks. You can also use this kick-off meeting to hand out study guides, spend some time getting to know each other, discuss each person's expectations for the group and briefly pray for each other. A simple meal or good desserts always make a kick-off meeting more fun.

After people introduce themselves and share how they ended up being at the meeting (you can play a game to see who has the wildest story!), have everyone respond to a few icebreaker questions:

- What is your favorite family vacation?
- What is one thing you love about your church/our community?

- What are three things about your life growing up that most people here don't know?

Next, ask everyone to tell what he or she hopes to get out of the study. You might want to review the Small Group Agreement and talk about each person's expectations and priorities.

Finally, set an open chair (maybe two) in the center of your group and explain that it represents someone who would enjoy or benefit from this group but who isn't here yet. Ask people to pray about inviting someone to join the group over the next few weeks. Hand out postcards and have everyone write an invitation or two. Don't worry about ending up with too many people; you can always have one discussion circle in the living room and another in the dining room after you watch the lesson. Each group could then report prayer requests and progress at the end of the session.

You can skip this kick-off meeting if your time is limited, but you'll experience a huge benefit if you take the time to connect with each other in this way.

# LEADING FOR THE
# FIRST TIME

- **Sweaty palms are a healthy sign.** The Bible says God is gracious to the humble. Remember who is in control; the time to worry is when you're not worried. Those who are soft in heart (and sweaty palmed) are those whom God is sure to speak through.

- **Seek support.** Ask your leader, co-leader, or close friend to pray for you and prepare with you before the session. Walking through the study will help you anticipate potentially difficult questions and discussion topics.

- **Bring your uniqueness to the study.** Lean into who you are and how God wants you to uniquely lead the study.

- **Prepare. Prepare. Prepare.** Go through the session several times. If you are using the DVD, listen to the teaching segment and Leadership Lifter. Consider writing in a journal or fasting for a day to prepare yourself for what God wants to do. Don't wait until the last minute to prepare.

- **Ask for feedback so you can grow.** Perhaps in an email or on cards handed out at the study, have everyone write down three things you did well and one thing you could improve on. Don't get defensive. Instead, show an openness to learn and grow.

- **Prayerfully consider launching a new group.** This doesn't need to happen overnight, but God's heart is for this to take place over time. Not all Christians are called to be leaders or teachers, but we are all called to be "shepherds" of a few someday.

- **Share with your group what God is doing in your heart.** God is searching for those whose hearts are fully his. Share your trials and victories. We promise that people will relate.

- **Prayerfully consider whom you would like to pass the baton to next week.** It's only fair. God is ready for the next member of your group to go on the faith journey you just traveled. Make it fun, and expect God to do the rest.

# LEADERSHIP TRAINING
# 101

Congratulations! You have responded to the call to help shepherd Jesus' flock. There are few other tasks in the family of God that surpass the contribution you will be making. As you prepare to lead, whether it is one session or the entire series, here are a few thoughts to keep in mind. We encourage you to read these and review them with each new discussion leader before he or she leads.

1. **Remember that you are not alone.** God knows everything about you, and He knew that you would be asked to lead your group. Remember that it is common for all good leaders to feel that they are not ready to lead. Moses, Solomon, Jeremiah and Timothy were all reluctant to lead. God promises, "Never will I leave you; never will I forsake you" (Hebrews 13:5). Whether you are leading for one evening, for several weeks, or for a lifetime, you will be blessed as you serve.

2. **Don't try to do it alone.** Pray right now for God to help you build a healthy leadership team. If you can enlist a co-leader to help you lead the group, you will find your experience to be much richer. This is your chance to involve as many people as you can in building a healthy group. All you have to do is call and ask people to help. You'll probably be surprised at the response.

3. **Just be yourself.** If you won't be you, who will? God wants you to use your unique gifts and temperament. Don't try to do things

exactly like another leader; do them in a way that fits you! Just admit it when you don't have an answer, and apologize when you make a mistake. Your group will love you for it, and you'll sleep better at night!

4. **Prepare for your meeting ahead of time.** Review the session and the leader's notes, and write down your responses to each question. Pay special attention to exercises that ask group members to do something other than engage in discussion. These exercises will help your group live what the Bible teaches, not just talk about it. Be sure you understand how an exercise works, and bring any necessary supplies (such as paper and pens) to your meeting. If the exercise employs one of the items in the appendices, be sure to look over that item so you'll know how it works. Finally, review "Outline for Each Session" so you'll remember the purpose of each section in the study.

5. **Pray for your group members by name.** Before you begin your session, go around the room in your mind and pray for each member by name. You may want to review the prayer list at least once a week. Ask God to use your time together to touch the heart of every person uniquely. Expect God to lead you to whomever He wants you to encourage or challenge in a special way. If you listen, God will surely lead!

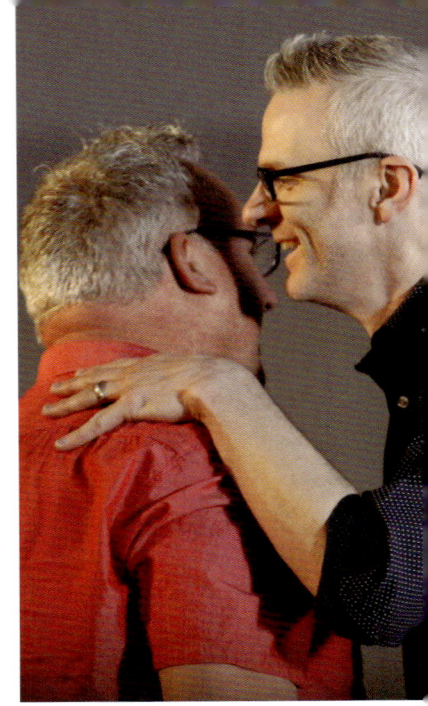

6. **When you ask a question, be patient.** Someone will eventually respond. Sometimes people need a moment or two of silence to think about the question. Keep in mind, if silence doesn't bother you, it won't bother anyone else. After someone responds, affirm the response with a simple "thanks" or "good job." Then ask, "How about somebody else?" or "Would someone who hasn't shared like to add anything?" Be sensitive to new people or reluctant members who aren't ready to say, pray or do anything. If you give them a safe setting, they will blossom over time.

7. **Provide transitions between questions.** When guiding the discussion, always read aloud the transitional paragraphs and the questions. Ask the group if anyone would like to read the paragraph or Bible passage. Don't call on anyone, but ask for a volunteer, and then be patient until someone begins. Be sure to thank the person who reads aloud.

8. **Break up into smaller groups each week.** If your group has more than seven people, we strongly encourage you to have the group gather sometimes in discussion circles of three or four people during the Growing Together or Sharing Together sections of the study. With a greater opportunity to talk in a small circle, people will connect more with the study, apply more quickly what they're learning and ultimately get more out of it. A small circle also encourages a quiet person to participate and tends to minimize the effects of a more vocal or dominant member. It can also help people feel more loved in your group. When you gather again at the end of the section, you can have one person summarize the highlights from each circle. Small circles are also helpful during prayer time. People who are unaccustomed to praying aloud will feel more

comfortable trying it with just two or three others. Also, prayer requests won't take as much time, so circles will have more time to actually pray. When you gather back with the whole group, you can have one person from each circle briefly update everyone on the prayer requests. People are more willing to pray in small circles if they know that the whole group will hear all the prayer requests.

9. **Rotate facilitators weekly.** At the end of each meeting, ask the group who should lead the following week. Let the group help select your weekly facilitator. You may be perfectly capable of leading each time, but you will help others grow in their faith and gifts if you give them opportunities to lead. You can use the Small Group Calendar to fill in the names of all meeting leaders at once if you prefer.

10. **One final challenge for new or first time leaders:** Before your first opportunity to lead, look up each of the five passages listed below. Read each one as a devotional exercise to help yourself develop a shepherd's heart. Trust us on this one. If you do this, you will be more than ready for your first meeting.

**MATTHEW 9:36**
**1 PETER 5:2-4**
**PSALM 23**
**EZEKIEL 34:11-16**
**1 THESSALONIANS 2:7-8, 11-12**

GRACE HAPPENS

40 DAYS OF GRACE